AT BATTLE IN THE REVOLUTIONARY WAR

AN INTERACTIVE BATTLEFIELD ADVENTURE

by Elizabeth Raum

Consultant:
Len Travers
Associate Professor of History
University of Massachusetts Dartmouth

CAPSTONE PRESS
a capstone imprint

You Choose Books are published by Capstone Press,
1710 Roe Crest Drive, North Mankato, Minnesota 56003
www.capstonepub.com

Library of Congress Cataloging-in-Publication Data
Raum, Elizabeth.
At battle in the revolutionary war : an interactive battlefield adventure / by Elizabeth Raum.
pages cm. — (You choose books. You choose: battlefields)
Summary: "In You Choose format, explores the Revolutionary War from the perspectives of colonists, British soldiers, militia soldiers, and foreigners"—Provided by publisher.
Includes bibliographical references and index.
ISBN 978-1-4914-2150-5 (library binding)
ISBN 978-1-4914-2392-9 (paperback)
ISBN 978-1-4914-2396-7 (eBook PDF)
1. United States. Continental Army—Military life—Juvenile literature.
2. Great Britain. Army—Military life—History—18th century—Juvenile literature.
3. Soldiers—United States—History—18th century—Juvenile literature. 4. Soldiers—Great Britain—History—18th century—Juvenile literature. 5. United States—History—Revolution, 1775-1783—Juvenile literature. I. Title.
E259.R38 2015
973.7—dc23 2014023848

Editorial Credits
Mari Bolte, editor; Tracy Davies McCabe, designer; Wanda Winch, media researcher; Laura Manthe, production specialist

Photo Credits
Bridgeman Images: ©Look and Learn/Private Collection/C.L. Doughty, 42, Peter Newark American Pictures/Private Collection, 16; Courtesy of Army Art Collection, U.S. Army Center of Military History, 31; Getty Images: Stock Montage, 8, UIG/Prisma, 45; Library of Congress: Prints and Photographs Division, 23, 73, 100, 102; National Archives and Records Administration, 66; New York Public Library: Astor, Lenox and Tilden Foundations, Miriam and Ira D. Wallach Division of Art, Prints and Photographs, Emmet Collection, 21; North Wind Picture Archives, 6, 12, 18, 57, 88; Pamela Patrick White, www.ppatrickwhite.com, cover, 49, 83; SuperStock: SuperStock, 27; Tennessee State Museum, Tennessee Historical Society Collection, 79; Werner Willis Fine Art, 74; www.historicalimagebank.com, Painting by Don Troiani, 37, 63, 96

Printed in Canada.
092014 008478FRS15

1

THE WAR FOR INDEPENDENCE

The year 1765 is a time of change in the 13 American colonies. Great Britain still rules, appointing governors, making laws, and stationing soldiers. But the government also gives the colonists a voice. Communities are allowed to hold town meetings to elect local officials. They can elect representatives to colonial assemblies. These assemblies make laws and resolve property disputes. They discuss the future of the colonies.

After several wars in the colonies against France, Great Britain's King George III raises taxes. Keeping the colonies safe is expensive. The king expects the colonists to help with the costs.

Turn the page.

The colonists don't see it that way. They hold protests and boycotts, refusing to buy British products. The colonists in Massachusetts, led by Samuel Adams and John Hancock, do not accept laws made by the British governor.

King George sends more soldiers to Boston. On March 5, 1770, British soldiers fire into a disruptive crowd, killing five colonists. Patriot Samuel Adams calls this the Boston Massacre.

The Boston Massacre was also known as the "State Street Massacre" and the "Bloody Massacre in King Street."

More protests follow. On December 16, 1773, colonists dump British tea into Boston Harbor. The event becomes known as the Boston Tea Party. The governor, Thomas Hutchinson, is outraged. He asks Great Britain for more troops to help control the rebels.

The colonists will not be controlled. They organize the First Continental Congress. Every colony except Georgia sends a representative. At the meeting in Philadelphia in 1774, the Congress asks Great Britain to respect the colonists' rights of self-government. Their plea is ignored. In fact, the situation gets worse.

More laws are passed to control the colonists. The colonists prepare for war. Men join the local militia groups and begin to stockpile weapons and ammunition.

Turn the page.

British leaders try to maintain order. Thomas Gage, the new military governor of Massachusetts, threatens those who rebel. Many families flee Boston and nearby Charlestown.

Gage orders elite British soldiers to march from Boston to Lexington and Concord. In Lexington they will capture the famous patriot leaders Samuel Adams and John Hancock. In Concord they are to seize gunpowder, cannons, and other weapons.

In the early hours of April 19, 1775, the British soldiers arrive in Lexington. But word has spread, and militiamen wait for them. Guns go off. No one knows who fired first, but that shot becomes known as "the shot heard 'round the world."

By the end of the day, 73 British soldiers and 49 patriot militiamen are dead. Others are wounded or missing. The war for independence has begun.

Everyone is touched by the war, including you. You have the opportunity to participate in three major battles. Which will you choose?

To fight with the Massachusetts militia or as a British regular at the Battle of Bunker Hill, turn to page 13.

To witness the Battle of Saratoga as an English nanny or a drummer boy, turn to page 43.

To join the fight at King's Mountain with the Overmountain Men or the loyalist militia, turn to page 75.

The Battle of Bunker Hill was a fight between inexperienced patriot militiamen and professional British soldiers.

2

BOSTON'S BUNKER HILL

Boston in 1775 is an armed camp. Most of the original 15,000 residents have left the city. Those who remain are either British-supporting loyalists or residents who are unable to leave.

Nearly 9,000 British soldiers, called regulars, are camped in the city. Battleships are anchored in the port of Boston. The most important British generals arrived in May to advise the governor of the Massachusetts Colony.

Thousands of militiamen are camped across the river. They are armed and ready to fight.

The battle is about to begin.

To fight with the Massachusetts militia, turn to page 14.

To fight as a British regular, turn to page 19.

On April 20 an alarm rider speeds past your farm shouting, "To arms!"

You grab your musket and the pouch sling that hangs nearby. The pouch holds several paper cartridges tied at both ends. Each one is stuffed with gunpowder and a musket ball.

You join some minutemen at Worcester Common. Minutemen are militiamen trained to report for duty in short notice. "Ready in a minute," one says with a smile, "and off to battle."

It's a two-day march to Cambridge. Once there, you set up camp, drill, clean your musket, and wait. By mid-June militiamen from all over New England have joined you.

Soon it will be past planting season. Your wife, Hannah, cannot tend the farm alone.

"I'm a farmer, not a fighter," you say to your friend Elias.

"This fight is about our families, our farms, and our way of life!" Elias counters. His words are a powerful reminder of why you joined the militia.

The atmosphere in the camp has changed. The captain orders you to assemble on the Cambridge Common at 6:00 that night.

Colonel William Prescott is in charge. Several wagons contain shovels, picks, empty barrels, and cages filled with dirt and rocks called gabions. "Looks like dirty work," Elias says.

You look down at your homespun clothing, filthy from weeks of camping on the Common. There is no official uniform. Each man carries his own weapon. Most, including you, have muskets. Some have axes or tomahawks.

"This way," a commanding officer barks. "We're going up Bunker Hill."

Turn the page.

It takes time for 1,000 men to cross narrow Charlestown Neck. The neck is only 30 feet wide in some places. It crosses the Charles River causeway and connects Charlestown to Boston. During high tide, the strip of land is underwater, but even then ships cannot get too close. After you cross, you make your way up Bunker Hill.

A causeway prevented ships from getting within 1,500 feet of Charlestown Neck.

When you reach the summit, the officers call a halt. Lieutenant Colonel Prescott, General Israel Putnam, and Lieutenant Gridley are arguing. Gridley is an engineer. Two of the officers want to follow orders and build a fort on Bunker Hill. But Gridley insists on going to Breed's Hill, half a mile southeast. He wins.

"It's a wise decision," Elias whispers. "From Breed's Hill our cannons can strike British ships in the harbor."

"The British can strike us too," you say with far less enthusiasm.

Prescott plans to build an earthen fort called a redoubt on Breed's Hill. Gridley is in charge. "Extend the walls 132 feet in both directions to form a V. Leave a small opening in the rear. It will be the only way in or out of the redoubt. The sun rises at 4:00. Get to work, men!"

Turn the page.

You get to work. You must dig down several feet and use that dirt to build walls. The empty barrels, gabions, and bundles of brushwood support the earthen walls.

Prescott calls, "I need sharpshooters to stand sentry at Charlestown. Any volunteers?"

You're tempted to volunteer, but Elias puts a hand on your arm. "Sentry duty is dangerous. I'm staying here."

Building the redoubt was backbreaking work.

To stay at the redoubt, turn to page 26.

To serve as a sentry, turn to page 29.

The boom of a cannon wakes you. You crawl out of your tent, one of hundreds on Boston Common. "What's happening?" you ask your friend Jasper Andrews.

"I don't know. I was sleeping when I heard cannon fire."

"Me too. I wonder what it could be about?" you say.

"Word from the ship captains is that the rebels are digging a fort on Breed's Hill. The watch on one of the ships saw them," someone tells you. "Then they started firing." The cannonballs hiss as they sail toward their targets.

You prepare for battle. You polish your musket, a British Brown Bess, and sharpen the bayonet attached to the end. You dress in your red uniform, white breeches, black boots, and a tricorn hat.

Turn the page.

The captain orders all British regulars to report for duty. "The tide comes in around 1:00. We'll march to Long Wharf and take boats to Morton's Point. General William Howe and Brigadier Robert Pigot are in command."

Ferrying all 1,500 regulars across the water in longboats takes nearly an hour. You gather on the beach. Heavy cannons on Copp's Hill provide cover. "Form companies!" a captain shouts.

Cannon fire bursts from two British ships floating in the harbor, the *Lively* and the *Falcon*. Two more, the *Glasgow* and the *Symmetry*, aim their cannons at nearby Charlestown. Although the ships are anchored in the middle of the harbor, their guns are still deadly. Both can hit targets up to 1,800 yards away.

Bang! A musket ball whizzes past your head. Snipers must be shooting from Charlestown.

The captain points up the hill. "We're to advance on the redoubt, that big earthen fort."

You take your place in the long row of redcoats. At the captain's order, you march forward. Great pyramids of fire rise above Charlestown. "We're burning Charlestown!" Jasper shouts. The 300 or so buildings in the abandoned city send plumes of smoke into the sky. "That will stop the snipers," he says.

When finished the redoubt measured more than 70 feet long and over 6 feet high.

Turn the page.

The cannons on your side have stopped firing, and an eerie quiet takes over. "They can't risk hitting us," Jasper says. You march up the hillside, slipping on the soggy, uneven ground. A breastwork and fences bar the way.

When you're in musket range, the captain orders a charge. You thrust the 17-inch-long bayonet blade forward. "Bellow as loudly as you can," the captain says. "They'll run at the sight and sound of you." You're skeptical, and the thought of running toward the redoubt is frightening. But you do it anyway.

You're almost to the breastwork when the rebels open fire. Two men on your left fall. An officer sinks to the ground. "I'm hit!" he yells.

"Retreat!" the captain orders.

To retreat as ordered, go to page 23.

To help the officer, turn to page 31.

Blood gushes from the officer's leg. He won't survive. There's no point in stopping and there's no time to grieve. You retreat beyond the range of rebel muskets, down the hill about 100 yards.

Brigadier Pigot calls, "Form lines!" The men fall in and make neat rows. You're in the sixth row from the front.

"Forward!"

General Howe believed the patriot soldiers would flee when faced with waves of British soldiers swarming toward them.

Turn the page.

The ground is rough and littered with logs and debris. You stumble in the tall grass and bump into the fences. Your legs ache more each time you pick yourself up off the ground. Pigot orders you to remove your heavy packs. Then he spurs you on.

Finally, you are within 50 yards of the rebels. They are hiding behind the redoubt. You take a breath. Confidence surges through you. When you charge, they'll run.

Suddenly, the rebels open fire. Musket balls rain down on you. Several officers fall. The rebels must be aiming for the fine red coats of the officers!

"Fall back!" the captain shouts.

And once more you retreat 50 yards down the hill.

"Reform your lines!" the captain commands. A rough line forms.

"Forward!" the captain orders.

Smoke fills the air. Musket fire is constant. The men at the front are invisible, hidden by smoke. A man in front of you falls. There's an opening in the line.

To stay in formation, turn to page 34.

To rush into the opening, turn to page 35.

"I'll stay too," you tell Elias.

You dig all night. At sunrise you look around. The rising sun reveals how close you are to British-held Boston. At least eight British ships float in the harbor. A red dot appears in the side of one of the ships. A deafening roar follows.

"Cannon fire!" someone yells. The iron ball lands with a sickening splat in the dirt behind you. Another follows. And another. You cower behind the earthen walls of the fort.

"Get to work!" an officer yells. "Cannons are noisy, but they rarely kill."

Seconds later a cannonball proves him wrong when the man next to you is hit and killed. The soldiers nearby gather around the body. But it's too late for Asa Pollard. His friends insist on a brief ceremony and bury him where he fell.

Colonel Prescott leaps onto the fort's wall. "Hit me if you can!" he shouts to the distant battleship. He encourages the men to keep working on the redoubt wall.

The sun is intense. "I'm hot and thirsty," Elias complains. There has been no food or rest since you arrived. And there is no water. One of the British ships destroyed the water supply with a cannonball earlier that day.

Colonel Prescott knew his men were tired and unprepared. He did what he could to help them feel less afraid before the battle.

Turn the page.

Suddenly, British cannons begin firing on you from Copp's Hill. "They'll kill us all!" one man says. He and several other men take off.

"Deserters," Elias says with disgust. While you don't intend to desert, you understand their fear. Many of them are farmers like you. This is the first battle for most of you.

By noon you finish the redoubt. Colonel Putnam arrives on his horse. He wants to build another fort on Bunker Hill. Colonel Prescott disagrees. He has watched the deserters and knows many men feel as though the battle is already over. "If you send the men away with tools, not one of them will return."

"Every man shall return," Putnam says, and then he asks for volunteers.

To go with Putnam, turn to page 32.

To stay with Prescott, turn to page 36.

You're a good marksman. You volunteer to go to Charlestown. Colonel Prescott sends the volunteers down the hillside. "Patrol the waterfront in shifts. Do not shut your eyes."

Charlestown is a ghost town. The nearly 300 houses and businesses stand empty. The owners fled when the governor threatened to burn the city to the ground if the militia entered.

Several British battleships float only a few hundred yards away. You see the watchman aboard the *Lively* stare in the direction of the digging men. Then he disappears. You wonder if he knows what is going on.

As the sun rises, distant ships in the harbor change from shadows to solid figures. You count five of them, all equipped with cannons. Each cannon requires a team of men to load and fire. The largest cannon requires a 14-man team.

Turn the page.

A dot of flame erupts from the *Lively*. An ear-shattering roar and the hiss of the cannonball follow.

"Run! Take cover!" a sentry yells.

You duck into an empty house. Two others join you. "Where are the officers?" one asks. "What are we to do?"

"Stay here," one man says. "That was our last order. We should follow it."

"No, we should return to the redoubt," says another. "They'll need our help."

To remain in Charlestown, turn to page 33.

To return to the redoubt, turn to page 36.

You stop to help. Blood gushes from the officer's leg. "Lean on me," you tell him.

The officer shakes his head. "Leave me," he says. "Today we fight, conquer, or die!" His head sinks to the grass. His leg injury is serious, but men have survived worse. If you can get him to safety, he may recover. Rebel fire is constant. The bodies of the dead and dying surround you.

More than 1,050 British soldiers were killed or injured during the battle. Patriot casualties were around 440—with most occurring during the retreat.

Turn to page 40.

You volunteer to go to Bunker Hill. You hate digging, but at least you'll be farther from the British forces. Colonel Putnam rides from one end of the hill to the other. Nobody knows if you're supposed to be attacking or building. Cannons roar in the harbor behind you, and the air is filled with smoke.

Colonel John Stark's men are fresh and ready for battle. They march off. You're left idle, waiting for orders. Sweat pours down your face. Where is Colonel Putnam? Who is in charge?

Men begin to leave. You and Elias join them. "At least we'll live to fight another day," Elias says.

"I would have stayed if Colonel Putnam had told us what to do," you say irritably. But your fight is over. It's time to get home to Hannah.

THE END

To follow another path, turn to page 11.

To read the conclusion, turn to page 101.

"Let's stay here and fight!" you yell.

Cannon fire continues all morning. The air is thick with smoke and the constant roar of cannons. It's not just the *Lively*; the *Glasgow, Symmetry,* and the much smaller *Falcon* and *Spitfire* are firing too.

There's a lull mid-afternoon. Reinforcements arrive. "Prescott sent us," one man says. "The British are landing."

"We can pick them off from here," you say, aiming your musket toward the beach just below Breed's Hill. You fire and reload. You're fast. You can get off about three shots a minute.

The musket is noisy, and you're focused on shooting. But then another patriot pulls you outside. "The British are burning Charlestown!" he yells. "Run for your life!"

Turn to page 41.

You stay in line like you've been trained. An orderly attack is the rule.

Black smoke fills the air. The blast of muskets and cannons is deafening. The soldiers ahead of you climb the walls of the fort with bayonets drawn, but the rebels keep firing, killing your comrades. You're hot, sweaty, and angry. It's time to claim victory.

Suddenly the rebels stop firing. Is it possible? Have they run out of ammunition?

You surge forward, bayonet drawn. Your goal? Destroy the rebels. You lash out with your bayonet. It sinks into a target. You pull it back and attack again. Finally the smoke clears. The battle is over. Hundreds lay dead. But you've won.

THE END

To follow another path, turn to page 11.

To read the conclusion, turn to page 101.

You rush into the opening, stepping on the bodies of those who went before you. You climb the earthen wall of the redoubt, musket in hand. As you peer down into the ditch, a rebel raises his musket and fires.

"My leg!" you scream and fall to the ground moaning. Others climb over you. Eventually your comrades carry you to a makeshift hospital.

It's late summer by the time you return to London. You and 170 other wounded soldiers make the journey across the Atlantic on the *Charming Nancy*. You're luckier than many. You survived the Battle of Bunker Hill.

THE END

To follow another path, turn to page 11.

To read the conclusion, turn to page 101.

You choose the redoubt. It's a dangerous choice. "We're fighting for freedom! We have to defend Breed's Hill," you declare.

"The British are burning Charlestown, ships are bombarding us, the regulars are surging toward us, and we're running out of ammunition!" Elias counters.

You peer down at the British troops. They landed on the beach and formed orderly lines. The lines are deep, with many rows of soldiers. If you kill those in front, more will follow. There seem to be thousands of them and only about

150 of you defending the redoubt. With luck, the swampy land and breastwork barriers will slow the enemy down.

"Stop shooting!" Prescott orders. Officers run along the top of the redoubt knocking the musket muzzles up so you can't fire.

The patriot soldiers waited until the British troops were close before firing.

"You're wasting ammunition," an officer explains. "Don't fire until you can see the buttons on their jackets." That makes sense. Muskets only have an accurate range of about 75 yards.

"Form teams!" You team up with Elias and another man. Two will reload while the other shoots. Each of you should get off three shots per minute.

Turn the page.

The regulars surge toward you. You fire. They fall back. But they reorganize and strike again.

You fire, reload, and fire again. The constant blasts of the muskets deafen you. Smoke clouds the air. It's hard to see. Some men run out of ammunition. They start throwing anything they can find—metal, rocks, wood.

Elias finds an artillery cartridge on the ground and shares it with the men.

"Make every shot count," Prescott says.

British soldiers are climbing the redoubt. You shoot one and another comes. Is there no end to them? "More gunpowder!" you yell.

But there is no more. The British regulars, bayonets drawn, surge over the redoubt.

To keep fighting, go to page 39.

To retreat, turn to page 41.

A British soldier leaps over the wall, bayonet drawn. "Watch out!" Elias yells. You grab your musket and swing it like a sword, but the British soldier plunges his bayonet into your chest. The shiny buttons on his bright red coat wink at you as you die.

THE END

To follow another path, turn to page 11.

To read the conclusion, turn to page 101.

"Jasper!" you yell. "The lieutenant's been hit. Help me."

Jasper hesitates for a split second before joining you. He helps you drag the injured officer downhill. The officer moans when you stumble. "Push on," he whispers. "Fight, conquer, or die ... "

Jasper staggers and falls. He lets go of the lieutenant. He's been hit too!

You turn to run, but it's too late. A musket ball tears into your back. You die on the hillside far from home, beside the lieutenant and your good friend Jasper Andrews.

THE END

To follow another path, turn to page 11.

To read the conclusion, turn to page 101.

You're nearly out of ammunition. The British have plenty. They also have deadly bayonets for close fighting. It's retreat or die. You race toward Charlestown Neck, stop, crouch behind a fence, and fire. Then you run to the next fence, reload your musket, and fire before racing on.

It seems to take years to cover the few miles to the mainland. Finally, you reach safety. There's no disgrace in retreat, not after such a gallant fight. There will be another day and another battle. There will be other chances to defeat the British.

THE END

To follow another path, turn to page 11.

To read the conclusion, turn to page 101.

General Burgoyne leading troops to battle

3

THE BATTLE OF SARATOGA

British General John Burgoyne has developed a bold plan to end the war. He'll march south from Canada along Lake Champlain to the Hudson River Valley. General William Howe will march north from New York City. When the two British armies meet, New England will be separated from the rest of the colonies.

In June Burgoyne's army marches south. It includes 4,000 British regulars, 3,000 German soldiers—called Hessians—hired by the British, 400 American Indians from the Iroquois, Algonquian, Abenaki, and Ottawa tribes, 300 Canadian woodsmen, and 300 loyalists.

Turn the page.

The army also carries 138 pieces of artillery, including cannons, howitzers, and mortars. It's an impressive sight.

After capturing Fort Ticonderoga, Burgoyne's troops move toward Saratoga, New York. Colonial troops do everything they can to slow Burgoyne's progress. They block roads by cutting down trees, flooding creeks, and destroying bridges. They also destroy crops and scare away livestock, making it impossible for the huge British army to resupply. By the time Burgoyne arrives, his men are tired and hungry. General Howe and his troops are still in Pennsylvania. And Daniel Morgan's Riflemen and patriot militiamen, desperate for a victory, are waiting.

The major battle is about to begin.

To be an English nanny hired by a Hessian general, go to page 45.

To be a drummer boy in the Connecticut militia, turn to page 48.

Lady Frederike Von Riedesel greets you in perfect English. She introduces you to her two small children. You will be their nanny. Nancy, your sister, will serve as Lady Fritz's maid.

"My husband commands more than 4,000 of the 19,000 Brunswicker soldiers who fight in the colonies," Lady Fritz says. "We will join him there."

German troops were often lumped together as "Hessians," regardless of their origin. The Brunswickers were from Brunswick, in northern Germany.

Turn the page.

In mid-April of 1777, you set sail from Portsmouth, England. It takes you several more weeks to reach Quebec, Canada. But by the time you get there, you find the general has already left. "We'll follow him," Lady Fritz says.

Light, fast wagons called calashes take you to Berthieux, 15 miles away. From there you take a canoe to Three Rivers where General Von Riedesel waits.

It's a happy reunion, but the general can't stay long. In mid-August he rejoins his troops. The Lady travels more slowly with the children. At Fort Edward a German captain has news. "John Stark and his rebels surprised us at Bennington. Nine hundred of our men were killed or captured."

"And my husband?" Lady Fritz gasps.

"He is well. He's waiting for you at Freeman's Farm. It's on the Hudson River, near Saratoga."

When you reach Freeman's Farm, the Von Riedesels share a single room in General Burgoyne's headquarters. You and Nancy sleep in a small closet.

"The American General Philip Schuyler destroyed the harvest as he retreated. Our food supply is running low," the cook says. He tries to stretch what he has, but it is not enough. Lady Fritz gives her share to the children. You do too.

As you and Nancy prepare to do laundry, a friendly soldier mentions that there's an apple tree in the far meadow. "What a treat! I'll go pick some," you say.

"But what about the laundry?" Nancy asks.

To pick apples, turn to page 53.

To help Nancy with the laundry, turn to page 54.

"Victory at Bennington!" Town criers throughout Connecticut spread the news. The victory is an important one. It reduces both the British army's size and supplies.

Militia groups prepare to march to Saratoga. Captain Asa Bray leads your father's unit. "Can I go too?" you ask Father. "You need a drummer boy. I'm 13 and I know the signals." Drum beats can be heard over long distances and are how the army communicates in battle. Some drumbeats mean "attack." Others mean "withdraw."

Mother frowns. "War is not a child's game."

"But drummer boys are not soldiers. I won't carry a weapon."

Father shakes his head. "That won't matter if you're being shot at. But it is an important job. You'll be the one to signal the enemy for a meeting or a ceasefire. It's an honorable position."

Finally Mother gives in. Captain Bray welcomes you to the unit.

You wear your everyday clothes—a linen shirt and wool overalls. "Take your hunting frock," Mother says, handing you a heavy outer shirt. "The weather is getting cooler." She gives you a warm blanket for sleeping. You don't have shoes, so you wrap rags around your feet to protect them.

Drummer boys played in camps, while marching, or during battle.

Turn the page.

Father cleans and polishes his musket. You help Mother prepare ammunition. You fill paper cartridges with gunpowder and a musket ball. Father will wear them in an ammunition pouch strapped across his chest. He'll also carry a powder horn and cartridge boxes, a canteen, and a black ball of wax for waterproofing supplies. You carry a drum, a canteen, and your blanket.

A broad-brimmed felt hat protects you from the sun as you walk the 130 miles from Connecticut to Saratoga. In mid-September you reach patriot headquarters on Bemis Heights, which overlooks the Hudson River.

"Set up camp," Captain Bray orders. Father stretches canvas over a horizontal bar to form a wedge-shaped tent. Six of you will sleep here. As the nights get cooler, you're happy for the blanket from Mother.

Every day you drill, collect firewood, and haul water from a nearby brook. Sometimes you help make fire cakes, mixing flour, water, and salt together. Then you bake them on hot rocks next to the fire. They're not very tasty, but they keep you from being hungry.

"Burgoyne and his army are at Freeman's Farm, about a mile to the north," an officer reports one night. "Scouts estimate their numbers at 4,000."

"There are more of us," you boast. Then you're embarrassed for speaking out of turn—and to an officer!

But the officer smiles and agrees. "We have around 10,000 men, and more arrive every day. The numbers are on our side."

Turn the page.

News flies around the camp. "Major General Schuyler retreated south after Ticonderoga. But he was smart," one soldier says. "He burned the crops in the fields and destroyed bridges. There's more than one way to win a war!"

Another soldier tells you about the battle at Freeman's Farm. "The British fired the first shot. Lucky for us, Daniel Morgan's Riflemen didn't hesitate. They killed several British officers before British reinforcements arrived. The British claimed victory. They camped on the battlefield that night. But we'll beat them next time."

Orders arrive: Prepare for battle. You and Henry, an older boy, report for duty. "Colonel Morgan has no drummer," an officer says.

To go to Colonel Morgan, turn to page 55.

To stay with the Connecticut militia, turn to page 56.

Nancy can do the laundry alone. You're hungry and you know the children are too. You decide to gather apples. The colonists may have destroyed crops, but they didn't cut down the apple trees.

It's a lovely fall day. Dewey grass brushes your ankles as you cross the meadow. The apple tree is at the edge of a forest, and you can smell the sweet fruit. Dozens of apples have fallen to the ground. You gather the best ones in the folds of your skirt.

Suddenly, you hear the unmistakable boom of a cannon. The battle's begun!

To run to the house, turn to page 58.

To take cover in the woods, turn to page 59.

Nancy needs help. You'll gather apples later. Several children are playing near the brook where you wash clothes. Suddenly there's a loud boom. A little girl screams. The battle has started.

The battlefield is only an hour's walk away. The sounds of musket fire and cannon blasts pound your ears. Then soldiers arrive, carrying wounded officers. "The rebels aimed for their bright coats," one says.

You hear rumors that the British will retreat. But General Von Riedesel disagrees. And he is right. Several weeks later, Lady Fritz tells you the fighting is about to resume. "We will need more wood. Go quickly. Don't linger."

You don't linger. But you're in the woods when the shooting begins.

To stay safe in the woods, turn to page 59.

To run to the house, turn to page 67.

You're eager to help Colonel Morgan. He's a hero. So are his men, known as Morgan's Riflemen. Thick trees provide cover as you walk the mile or so to Freeman's Farm. In a field beyond the trees, several women and children are harvesting wheat for the horses. You realize you are surrounded by loyalists and British soldiers.

You notice an officer on horseback and British soldiers forming lines. They are preparing for battle! Your path is blocked.

To return to Headquarters, turn to page 61.

To find Colonel Morgan, turn to page 63.

Henry jumps at the chance to help the famous rifleman. You're happy to stay where you are. "We'll follow General Enoch Poor into battle. He's a Massachusetts man," Father says.

It's late morning when you hear a cannon fire. You beat out the message, "Assemble for battle." Then you march out. You hear Morgan's Riflemen shooting in the distance.

General Poor leads you to a field surrounded by yellow pines near Freeman's Farm. British troops stand in line with their artillery in front. On orders, you drum, "Commence firing." Guns go off. Smoke fills the air. A British general on horseback tumbles to the ground.

General Benedict Arnold gallops up and down the line of patriot militiamen waving his sword in the air and urging men to fight. "We're going forward," Captain Bray says.

Arnold has found an opening in the British defense near Breymann Redoubt. But the opening is not clear. German troops stand between the redoubt and two small cabins nearby.

Patriot and German muskets exchange fire. The Germans run for their lives. A bullet strikes General Arnold in the leg. Another kills his horse. The general falls a few yards from you.

Benedict Arnold was shot in the right leg. His horse fell on the wounded leg when it was killed, further injuring Arnold.

To rush to the general's aid, turn to page 70.

To stay at your post, turn to page 71.

You race back to Freeman's Farm. General Von Riedesel rushes out. Lady Fritz follows him, distressed. "The battle rages," she says, shivering with every shot.

A short time later, three officers are carted into the house, all seriously wounded.

Nancy brushes past you toward a young soldier. "You're safe!" she cries. "I was so worried." She rushes into his arms. Then she turns to you. "Come out and meet Joseph," she says.

Lady Fritz is calling you from inside the house. It sounds like she needs help.

To go to Lady Fritz, turn to page 67.

To meet Joseph, turn to page 69.

Cannons boom in the distance. Are they close? You feel safe in the woods. You sit down on a mossy rock near a large tree.

The shooting seems to go on forever. You put your hands over your ears, close your eyes, and dream of your home in England.

When the shooting finally stops, you stand up. Where are you? It's dark now. You begin walking, but the farther you go, the more lost you feel. Finally, you see a light. A house!

It doesn't look familiar, but you have no choice. You knock.

A woman answers. "Yes?"

"I'm lost."

"You're English?" She lets you in.

Turn the page.

The woman introduces herself as Mrs. Coulson. She's a loyalist, and she's eager to help. "We hear that the colonists won the battle. If we return you to Saratoga, you'll become a prisoner of war. Stay with us instead."

"But what about my sister?"

"I fear we cannot help her."

The Coulsons get you to Canada where you find work as a nanny. You like Canada and stay there. Several years later you learn that Nancy returned to Germany with Lady Fritz. She is well and happy, and has married a Hessian soldier. You are grateful you both survived the war.

THE END

To follow another path, turn to page 11.

To read the conclusion, turn to page 101.

Patriot General Horatio Gates' headquarters sit on the bluff above the west bank of the Hudson River. Thick woods surround it. Deep ravines lead to the river. Strong breastworks protect the area from attack. Every few feet, there are spaces for cannons.

You race to the headquarters. "The British are forming a line near the wheat field!" you shout. But as you speak, gunfire echoes in the distance.

"Stay here," an officer barks. "We have work for you." You're relieved. It seems a lot safer here.

The battle rages outside. Smoke rises from the wheat field. Muskets blast constantly. Artillerymen stand by their cannons, ready if needed. You're surprised that General Gates doesn't join his troops. He stays safe inside the fort. You see Benedict Arnold ride off.

Turn the page.

Two men return to headquarters. They are leading a horse carrying a wounded British officer. It's Major Ackland, head of the royal grenadiers. A musket ball tore through both his legs.

"He's a brave man," one of the soldiers says. "Even though he fights for the other side, we had to help him."

"And the battle?"

"The British are retreating."

This seems like an important turning point in the war. The British have surrendered. They are working out the terms with General Gates. Six hundred of their troops and 150 of yours lie dead or wounded. You're lucky you're not one of them—and you're lucky to be going home.

Turn to page 72.

You circle back, using the woods for cover. Shots ring out. Colonel Morgan will need you. You run, ducking behind trees. You're tempted to hide until the battle ends. No one would blame you.

The Battle of Saratoga was actually two battles. The first took place on September 17, 1777. The second was on October 7.

To hide in the woods, turn to page 64.

To keep going, turn to page 65.

You sink down behind the trees. Gunfire is continuous. Cannons boom in the distance, and you hear men scream. A slight breeze carries the smell of burning powder and something else. Is it blood?

Then you hear drums in the distance. The gunfire stops. It's a ceasefire. You stand up and run toward Colonel Morgan. You skirt around men whose faces are blackened by gun smoke. Others lay wounded on the ground. Morgan wears a buckskin shirt, a powder horn around his neck, and a felt-rimmed hat. "Colonel Morgan. I'm your drummer. I got lost."

He looks at you as though he knows you hid instead of fought. But then he sighs. "It's just as well. A battlefield is no place for a boy." He turns away. You know the battle is over.

Turn to page 72.

You run toward the gunfire. Maybe you can help! The air is smoky. You report to Colonel Morgan. He looks at you. "Stay close and out of the way. I won't need you. I don't use drums."

Morgan's men are excellent marksmen. They pick a target and aim carefully for it. Unlike muskets, their rifles are accurate for a distance of more than 200 yards. But rifles take longer to load than muskets. The best rifleman can fire only one shot every minute.

Morgan signals his men with a turkey call. The men know exactly what it means.

You notice a British general riding back and forth on a gray horse. "That's Simon Fraser," Morgan says. "Murphy!" he calls. He orders the young rifleman to climb a tree and shoot Fraser. This is unusual. Many find the shooting of officers wrong. But Morgan encourages it.

Turn the page.

Murphy's shot is accurate. Fraser falls to the ground, seriously wounded.

The loss of Fraser is a big hit to the British Army. They fall back. The patriots claim victory. Later, Father calls Murphy's shot "the most important shot of the rebellion."

THE END

Daniel Morgan and his Riflemen were credited for killing many British officers. Their deaths convinced both Indians and loyalists to desert the British army at Saratoga.

To follow another path, turn to page 11.

To read the conclusion, turn to page 101.

"There you are. I need your help," Lady Fritz says. You prepare beds and bandages for the wounded. You haul water and forage for food. More than two weeks pass, but you and Nancy are so busy you barely notice.

One day two Native Americans rush past you in full battle dress. "War!" they shout. Another battle is about to begin.

When you see soldiers carrying British General Simon Fraser on a stretcher, you know the battle is lost. Burgoyne must surrender. It takes days to work out the details.

"What will happen to us?" you ask.

"We are prisoners of war," Lady Fritz says.

But being part of a prisoner general's household is not so bad. You are treated much better than most of the common prisoners of war.

Turn the page.

You and the Von Riedesels travel to Albany, New York. You are personal guests of the patriot General Philip Schuyler. The general welcomes General Burgoyne too. As they meet you hear Burgoyne say, "Is it to me, who has done you so much injury, that you show so much kindness?"

"That is the fate of war," the patriot general replies. "Let us say no more about it."

You spend several months in America, moving from one place to another with the Von Riedesels. Eventually you and Nancy return to England. You never forget the Von Riedesels' kindness or the kindness of the patriot general who treated his enemies like friends.

THE END

To follow another path, turn to page 11.

To read the conclusion, turn to page 101.

Joseph is a private in the British Army. "We plan to marry," Nancy says.

But a few days later, Joseph becomes ill. The doctors are busy caring for the wounded, so Nancy nurses Joseph. He doesn't get better. Then Nancy develops a fever. You try to help, but you also catch the fever. You watch from your sickbed as Joseph dies. Then Nancy is gone. You know you will be next.

THE END

To follow another path, turn to page 11.

To read the conclusion, turn to page 101.

You rush forward to free the general. Two others place him on a litter and carry him back to headquarters. His leg is broken. But the battle is won. Soon after, the British surrender. You admire General Arnold. Without his help the Americans might have lost Saratoga, which proves to be a turning point of the war.

You return home in time to harvest the crops.

Turn to page 73.

Others rush forward to assist General Arnold. What a brave man!

You are at Captain Bray's side when the British retreat. Your drum beats a ceasefire. The battlefield is strewn with bodies. Some are patriots. Most are British.

The next day your father helps bury the dead. "You stay here," he says. "You've seen enough death already." And it is true. But you've seen heroes too. You count Captain Bray, Daniel Morgan, and Benedict Arnold heroes of American independence.

Turn to page 73.

It's a relief to return home. You reach Connecticut in time to finish the harvest. You may be called out again, but for the winter of 1777, you will remain safe at home with Mother and Father. You've seen enough of war to last a lifetime.

THE END

To follow another path, turn to page 11.

To read the conclusion, turn to page 101.

In 1780 you are shocked to learn that Benedict Arnold has been helping the British. "A traitor!" the papers accuse. Arnold escapes to British-held New York City. Later he moves to Canada, and then to London. How could a loyal, high-ranking patriot commit treason? Your disappointment runs deep. George Washington becomes your hero. So does Daniel Morgan. You never utter the name "Benedict Arnold" again.

THE END

Benedict Arnold (right) began giving the British information just a year and a half after Saratoga.

To follow another path, turn to page 11.

To read the conclusion, turn to page 101.

The Overmountain Men stayed out of the war for five years. But they went to war when their families and farms were threatened.

4

THE FIGHT AT KING'S MOUNTAIN

At first, most battles are fought in the north. But the war begins moving south in 1778.

In April 1780 British General Henry Clinton targets Charleston, South Carolina. Many colonists loyal to Britain, called loyalists, live there, but the town is being held by patriots.

Clinton's men slowly creep closer to the town. The patriots answer with gunfire. After a month of firing back and forth, the city surrenders.

Loyalists, who feel safer under the king's rule, rush to aid the British.

Turn the page.

Clinton sends Major Patrick Ferguson, a decorated British soldier born in Scotland, to recruit even more loyalists. "We come not to make war on women and children, but to relieve their distresses," Ferguson says. Many men enlist. The British feel confident. General Clinton thinks he has won South Carolina.

Patriots from Maryland, Delaware, and Virginia march toward South Carolina. On August 16, 1780, patriot and loyalist armies clash at the Battle of Camden. It is a disaster for the patriots. They lose 1,000 men. Hundreds more are taken prisoner. But the patriots do not give up.

Two days later a small patriot force surprises Ferguson at Musgrove's Mill. More than 220 men are killed, injured, or captured. Only a dozen patriots are lost.

British General Charles Cornwallis is angry. He says he will hang traitors and imprison anyone who opposes the British. Major Ferguson threatens the people of South Carolina—he says he will "hang their leaders and lay their country waste with fire and sword."

The Overmountain Men live on the western side of the Blue Ridge Mountains in North Carolina, Virginia, and Tennessee. They are fierce patriot fighters, experts on horseback and with rifles, knives, and tomahawks. They are willing to die for independence.

Two armies, one patriot and one loyalist, are about to clash. Everyone, except Major Ferguson, is a colonist.

To join the Overmountain Men, turn to page 78.

To join the loyalist militia, turn to page 81.

The entire family gathers in the clearing beside your small log cabin home. "Colonel Campbell needs us to fight the British," Pa says. "He's joining with Isaac Shelby and John Sevier and their militias. We Overmountain Men can help. Who will join me?"

"I'll go!" you say. Pa nods his approval. Your uncle, older brother, and three cousins will go too.

Ma and the younger children will stay home. Two or three men will protect them. Ma stops your horse, Thunder, before you leave. "I'm worried. What if you see someone you know on the other side?" Her brother and two sisters live in eastern Virginia. They are loyalists.

"I have to fight, Ma. It's the price of freedom."

"Freedom costs dearly," she says, shaking her head sadly as she lets go of Thunder's bridle.

On September 23, 1780, you follow the Overmountain Trail to Dunn's Meadow in Abingdon, Virginia. Many troops and Overmountain Men are already there. Lean, tough backwoodsmen, many of the Overmountain Men have long hair, beards, and carry rifles and powder horns. They wear hunting shirts and tomahawks hang from their belts. Several women have come too.

About 1,000 Overmountain Men marched toward King's Mountain.

Turn the page.

The next day you cross Roan Mountain toward Gilbert Town. It begins to rain as you set up camp. Torrential rains and thunder keep you in camp throughout the next day.

Pa brings news. "Ferguson is at King's Mountain. We must continue."

At dawn on October 7, you reach the banks of the Broad River. The horses are exhausted. So are the men. But Colonel Shelby yells, "I will not stop until night, if I follow Ferguson into Cornwallis' lines!" And so you push on, despite the brutal pouring rain.

At noon the sun comes out. Scouts report that Ferguson is camped just a few miles ahead. You notice a young boy fidgeting on horseback. He looks suspicious.

To report the boy, turn to page 84.

To ignore the boy, turn to page 86.

"Victory at Camden!" Father cries. "The war will end soon!" Father is a loyalist store owner. "Taxes are the cost of doing business," he tells you. "British shipping makes trade possible."

Not everyone agrees. Your cousins, who live in the mountain region called the backwaters, want independence. Father calls them rebels.

You joined the loyalist militia a year ago, soon after your 18th birthday. It's an honor to serve with Major Patrick Ferguson in North Carolina. Under his command you have become a fair shot. You don't have a regulation bayonet, but you do carry a sharp knife.

Every afternoon you search for food. You take what you find. The locals do not resist. Major Ferguson has made it clear: Support the British or he will release his army to attack. In two weeks' time, 500 men have joined the loyalist militia.

Turn the page.

Men tell stories of Ferguson's valor. He fought for the king during the Seven Years' War. He was wounded in the right arm and now fights with his left. And he invented the Ferguson Rifle. Your Brown Bess musket can fire three shots a minute, but the musket loses accuracy beyond 75 yards. The Ferguson is accurate for more than twice that distance.

In late September you move to King's Mountain. Ferguson establishes headquarters at the summit's plateau. Seventeen wagons form a semicircle. White tents dot the area. It's a big camp: 1,125 men according to the captain. Ferguson calls himself King of the Mountain. "No one will push me off!"

October is rainy, but the sun is out when it's your turn to stand guard. You settle under a large tree halfway down the mountain.

The other guards are out of sight, but you know they are there. If an enemy approaches, they'll shoot or call out. For now, all is quiet.

Suddenly you see a man in hunting gear. You stare into the forest. Then you see another man, and then a third. You lift your musket, squeeze off a shot, and race back to camp.

Guards and scouts watched for nearby enemy soldiers.

Turn to page 87.

You alert Colonel Hambright. "That boy looks suspicious, sir. Could he be a spy?"

The colonel studies the boy. "I know him. His brother supports the king." He orders his men to arrest the loyalist boy named John Ponder. He is carrying messages from Major Ferguson to General Cornwallis. You've helped catch a spy!

After some questioning, Ponder confirms Ferguson's position. "He looks splendid," the boy adds, "but he wears a checkered shirt over his uniform." Hambright tells his men to mark Ferguson with their rifles.

King's Mountain comes into view. Forests cover the northern slopes. You cannot see the enemy. The enemy cannot see you either.

"The plan is to surround their camp from all directions. The loyalists will be trapped. We'll fight until they surrender," Pa says. The men break into two units—left and right. Colonel Campbell leads the right. Colonel Hambright leads the left.

Hambright nods at you. "You did us a good turn back there," he says. "I'd be pleased to have you join my men."

To join Hambright, turn to page 90.

To stay with Campbell, turn to page 91.

Colonel Hambright notices the boy too. He arrests him and discovers messages between Ferguson and British headquarters. The boy confirms Ferguson's position. If you had said something, you would have been a hero.

Colonel Campbell says, "If the loyalists had any courage, they would fight for independence. Use your best judgment in battle. Fire, then take cover. Don't go far. We'll try again until we win. But if any of you, men or officers, are afraid, quit and go home. You have my permission."

You study the men around you. They look brave, but your hands are shaking. An older man next to you notices. "He means it, son. Someone has to watch the supplies and help the wounded. No one will think less of you if you stay here."

To follow Campbell to battle, turn to page 91.

To wait at the bottom of the hill, turn to page 94.

As you dash back to camp, you hear drums. They signal the men to assemble on the southwest corner of the ridge. You made the right choice to return. You tie evergreen boughs onto your cap. The branches identify you as a loyalist. The rebels put paper or cloth on theirs.

Devilish screams echo off the hillsides. "It's those Yelling Boys!" an officer says. "The Overmountain Men are coming! Fire when ready!"

The rebels struggle up the steep mountain. You fire down at them. Several fall.

Major Ferguson rides by on horseback. "Charge!" he yells. You grip your knife and charge downhill.

The rebels run. Some hide behind trees or rocks. You want to pursue, but Ferguson's whistle calls you back.

Turn the page.

You fire and charge as the rebels surge up the hill once again. Officers ride among you on horseback, slashing the rebels with their swords. And the rebels retreat again.

There's a third assault. The rebels run again. "We've got them!" a captain yells. "Finish them!"

But then you hear a noise. Is that Ferguson's whistle? Is he calling you back to the summit?

The patriots used the tactic of surprise during the Battle of King's Mountain. They were not discovered until the loyalists were already surrounded.

To return to the summit, go to page 89.

To follow the rebels, turn to page 93.

The commands are confusing. Some of the men race downhill after the rebels. Others, including you, return to the mountaintop. "Reform lines!" the captain says.

The rebels stream up the mountain. A sniper shoots the officer who ordered you to charge. All is smoke and confusion. A musket ball tears your ear. Another rips holes in your shirt. A huge mountain man rushes toward you. You aim your musket, ready to fire. But then you hesitate. Something about him seems familiar.

To hold back, turn to page 95.

To shoot, turn to page 99.

You follow Colonel Hambright and Major Chronicle. They lead their men up the steep northeastern corner of the mountain. "Face to the hill!" Major Chronicle yells. You yell and scream as you rush forward.

Heavy British fire falls like hail. Two men, not much older than you, fall at your feet. Dead? There's no time to react. "A little nearer to them, my brave men," an officer yells.

The ground is rough. You stumble over rocks and roots, shooting as you go. The loyalists charge, bayonets drawn. Robert Henry, who is only a year older than you, takes aim and fires at a loyalist. As he shoots, British bayonets pierce his hand and thigh.

To rush to Robert's aid, turn to page 97.

To take cover behind a tree, turn to page 98.

You don't want to leave your father and brother, so you follow Colonel Campbell around the base of the mountain. You remember Colonel Shelby's words: "Never shoot until you see an enemy, and never see an enemy without bringing him down."

British drums beat. A whistle blows. "That's Ferguson," someone says.

"Halt, dismount, and prepare to attack!" Colonel Campbell calls. "Here they are, my brave boys. Fight!"

War whoops, gunfire, and screams echo through the hills. Rifle smoke blinds you. You run uphill from tree to tree until you see flashing bayonets rushing toward you.

From behind a tree, you aim and fire, forcing the loyalists back to the mountaintop.

Turn the page.

Your brother Josh appears at your side. "We're not alone," he says. "Shelby's and Sevier's men are circling the enemy. Let's go!"

Smoke, shouting, and shooting confuse the loyalists. You surge forward. As you approach the summit, you stop, take aim, and shoot. An officer topples off his horse.

You rush forward as a loyalist runs toward you. He tosses his gun aside. What's happening?

To hesitate, turn to page 95.

To fire your weapon, turn to page 99.

You chase the retreating men, but the ground is rough. You stumble, fall, and roll into a large rock. You sit up, musket ready. A man pops out from behind the rock. He's wearing a piece of paper in his hat. He's a rebel! He leaps toward you, knife drawn. You fire your musket.

Too late! He knocks the muzzle aside and sinks his knife into your belly. As the smoke clears, he pockets his knife and dashes away. His war whoop is the last thing you hear.

THE END

To follow another path, turn to page 11.

To read the conclusion, turn to page 101.

The older man has seen many battles. And he's right. Someone has to watch the supplies. You stay behind when the men march off. Birds sing and leaves rustle in the wind, but there are no sounds of approaching battle. Just before 3:00 you hear shots and the beating of British drums. The shrill war whoops of patriots follow. Rifles blast. Wounded men scream. Who lives? Who dies? Why aren't you there? The battle rages for 65 minutes.

"We won," Pa says when he returns. "But Josh is hurt." Your brother will use a crutch for the rest of his life. You spend your life helping him farm. It's the least you can do for a war hero.

THE END

To follow another path, turn to page 11.

To read the conclusion, turn to page 101.

He comes at you. You flinch, about to run, when he grabs you in a bear hug. "What … ?"

"It's me, your cousin Matthew!" he says. "It's so wonderful to see a familiar face!"

"This is war," you reply. "Pick up your gun and fight." You feel him tense. "If you cannot, then let me go so that I can."

Your cousin backs away and then runs into the woods. You never see him again.

Turn the page.

When the last shot clears, Major Ferguson lies dead. So do 244 of his men. The patriots count 29 dead and 58 wounded. The bloodshed sickens you. You help bury the dead and care for the wounded. At battle's end, two armies, bloody and battered, return to their camps to prepare for whatever comes next.

THE END

Near the end of the battle, the loyalist troops were surrounded. Ferguson refused to surrender and was shot from his horse.

To follow another path, turn to page 11.

To read the conclusion, turn to page 101.

You rush to Robert's side.

"Did I get him?" Robert asks weakly.

"You did. Shot him clean through."

Robert is bleeding heavily. You pull the bayonet out of his thigh and struggle to free his hand. Finally, you pull him to safety. "Don't leave me," he begs.

You crouch behind a tree and begin firing. Bark flies from the tree, and your eyes fill with dust. You don't stop until the British retreat.

When the battle ends, you carry Robert into camp and tend his wounds. He'll survive, thanks to you. Pa brings more good news. "Ferguson is dead," he says. "The victory is ours!"

THE END

To follow another path, turn to page 11.

To read the conclusion, turn to page 101.

You hesitate. Robert is bleeding heavily. You don't know how to help. Colonel Hambright rushes over and pulls you down. "Take cover!" he yells. "And keep shooting!"

You've gone only a few steps when a musket ball slams into your back. You fall forward, dead before you hit the ground.

THE END

To follow another path, turn to page 11.

To read the conclusion, turn to page 101.

This is war. He's the enemy. You fire your rifle, and he falls to the ground dead. You turn away, but something nags at you. You stop and take a closer look. It's your cousin Matthew! You've just killed your own cousin.

You continue to fight, but the outcome no longer matters. You've killed a man, a man you knew and loved, a man whose family you'll have to face. You survive the battle and return home, never to reveal your terrible secret. It haunts you for the rest of your life.

THE END

To follow another path, turn to page 11.

To read the conclusion, turn to page 101.

George Washington took command of the Continental army on July 3, 1775.

5 BATTLE OUTCOMES

Bunker Hill, Saratoga, and King's Mountain were all important Revolutionary War battles.

Bunker Hill was one of the bloodiest. Before they ran out of ammunition, patriot muskets killed or wounded nearly half the British force of 2,200 soldiers. About 40 percent of British officers lost their lives. The patriots lost about 450 men in the battle.

The battle showed patriot leaders that they needed a strong commander and a well-trained and well-equipped army. George Washington was made Commander-in-Chief in 1775.

Around this time, British leaders decided to leave Boston; it was too isolated and hilly. They moved to New York and the Carolinas.

The Battle of Saratoga is considered one of the most significant victories in world history. France was finally convinced to enter the war against Great Britain. They sent money, ships, arms, and men.

British and Hessian losses numbered around 600. More than four-fifths of Burgoyne's officers were captured. Patriot casualties totaled 150.

General Burgoyne surrendered to General Gates at Saratoga on October 17, 1777.

The reinforcements General Burgoyne expected from Generals Howe and Clinton never arrived. Howe needed all his men as he moved against Philadelphia. Clinton did send help, but what he sent was too little, too late.

Until the Battle of King's Mountain, many loyalists had no doubt Great Britain would be victorious. The British recruited local loyalist militias to fight. The battle was between loyalist and patriot militias.

It appeared that the British would win the battle. But British Major Ferguson ordered his troops to pull back rather than pursue.

The battle lasted about an hour. Loyalist forces were eventually surrounded on the mountaintop. Ferguson's death forced them to surrender. Loyalists began to question the British army's superiority.

More than 200,000 colonists participated in the war. Many served for only a few months. Fighting close to home was an advantage. But the colonists had trouble getting needed supplies. Militias provided their own guns, but there were seldom uniforms. Food and gunpowder were always in short supply. The French helped the colonists replenish some of their meager supplies.

For the British, waging war 3,000 miles away created problems. It took weeks to send messages to England and back. Reinforcements and supplies had to arrive by ship. The British troops also had to face both the Continental army and the thousands of civilians willing to fight.

After the war the British generals returned to England. Howe, Clinton, and Burgoyne all gave excuses for Great Britain's defeat. Burgoyne never received another command.

War was messy. There were few doctors and almost no battlefield hospitals. Antibiotics, which prevent infections, did not exist then. Many wounded soldiers died of infection. Even more soldiers died of disease. Between 70 and 90 percent of the soldiers who lost their lives during the Revolutionary War died of disease.

Fought in 1781, Yorktown was the last major battle of the American Revolution. There, British General Charles Cornwallis surrendered. Two years later, the United States and Great Britain signed the Treaty of Paris, which recognized the colonies' independence.

During the eight-year-long war, about 19,000 patriots died of battle wounds or disease. The British lost about 26,000 men, including nearly 3,000 loyalists and 10,000 Hessians. The war was costly for everyone.

TIMELINE

1760—King George III becomes king of Great Britain.

1765—English Parliament passes the Stamp Act. Colonists protest the taxes.

1768—British troops arrive in Boston.

1770—Five colonists are shot and killed by British soldiers in Boston, Massachusetts. This event becomes known as the Boston Massacre.

1773—Patriots dump tea in Boston Harbor to protest British taxes.

1774—First Continental Congress meets in Philadelphia, Pennsylvania.

April 1775—First shots of war are fired at Lexington and Concord in Massachusetts.

June 17, 1775—British win the Battle of Bunker Hill.

July 1776—Large British force reaches New York harbor.

July 4, 1776—Declaration of Independence is signed.

August 16, 1777—Patriot victory at Bennington, Vermont.

September 19, 1777—British capture Philadelphia; patriots win the Battle of Freeman's Farm.

October 17, 1777—British General John Burgoyne surrenders at the Battle of Saratoga.

February 6, 1778—France allies with the colonies.

December 1778—British occupy Savannah, Georgia.

June 21, 1779—Spain allies with the colonies.

September 23, 1779—Patriot Captain John Paul Jones and his ship *Bonhomme Richard* defeat the British vessel *Serapis* off the coast of England in a naval battle.

May 1780—British occupy Charleston, South Carolina.

August 1780—Colonists are defeated at the Battle of Camden, South Carolina.

September 23, 1780—British Major John André is arrested, revealing Benedict Arnold as a traitor.

October 7, 1780—Colonists win the Battle of King's Mountain in South Carolina.

October 19, 1781—British surrender at Yorktown.

January 1782—British troops and loyalists begin leaving the colonies.

September 3, 1783—Treaty of Paris is signed, officially ending the Revolutionary War.

May 1787—Constitutional Convention begins in Philadelphia.

1789—George Washington becomes the first president of the United States.

OTHER PATHS TO EXPLORE

In this book you've seen three different battles from several points of view. Perspectives on history are as varied as the people who lived it. Seeing history from many points of view is an important part of understanding it.

Here are some ideas for other Revolutionary War points of view to explore:

- Many residents fled Charlestown, Massachusetts, after British Governor Thomas Gage threatened them for letting the militia enter the city. During the Battle of Bunker Hill, the town was burned to the ground. What would it be like to lose everything you own? How would you feel toward the British soldiers who burned your town? (Integration of Knowledge and Ideas)

- About 400 American Indians fought with the British at the Battles of Saratoga. How would their experiences differ from those of a regular soldier? (Key Ideas and Details)

- Most women who followed the troops did everyday tasks like cooking, cleaning, and preparing ammunition. They were called camp followers. Many brought babies and children with them. What would life have been like for a child among the camp followers? (Integration of Knowledge and Ideas)

READ MORE

Clarke, Gordon. *Significant Battles of the American Revolution*. New York: Crabtree Publishing Company, 2013.

Landau, Elaine. *The Boston Tea Party: Would You Join the Revolution?* Berkeley Heights, N.J.: Enslow Elementary, 2014.

Morey, Allan. *A Timeline History of the Declaration of Independence*. Minneapolis: Lerner Publication Company, 2015.

Smith-Llera, Danielle. *The Revolutionary War: A Chronology of America's Fight for Independence*. North Mankato, Minn.: Capstone Press, 2015.

INTERNET SITES

Use FactHound to find Internet sites related to this book. All of the sites on FactHound have been researched by our staff.

Here's all you do:
Visit *www.facthound.com*
Type in this code: 9781491421505

GLOSSARY

artillery (ar-TIL-uh-ree)—large guns, such as cannons or missile launchers, that require several soldiers to load, aim, and fire

bayonet (BAY-uh-net)—a long metal blade attached to the end of a musket or rifle

boycott (BOY-kot)—to refuse to buy or use a product or service to protest something believed to be wrong or unfair

breastwork (brest-WORK)—temporary fortification during a battle

Continental Congress (kahn-tuh-nen-tuhl KAHNG-gruhs)—leaders from the 13 original American Colonies who made up the American government from 1774 to 1789

deserter (di-ZURT-ur)—a military member who leaves duty without permission

governor (GUHV-urn-ur)—a person who controls a country or state

grenadier (gruh-NAH-dee-eer)—an elite British soldier, chosen for size and strength

Hessian (HESS-ee-uhn)—a German soldier hired by the British

howitzer (HOU-uht-sur)—a cannon that shoots explosive shells long distances

loyalist (LOI-uh-list)—a colonist who was loyal to Great Britain during the Revolutionary War

militia (muh-LISH-uh)—groups of volunteer citizens organized to fight, but who are not professional soldiers

minutemen (MIN-uht-MEN)—colonists who were ready and willing to fight at a moment's notice

redoubt (rih-DOUT)—a small fort made of dirt

regular (REG-yoo-luhr)—a professional British soldier

sentry (SEN-tree)—a guard

treason (TREE-zuhn)—the crime of betraying one's government

BIBLIOGRAPHY

Dameron, J. David. *King's Mountain: The Defeat of the Loyalists, October 7, 1780.* Cambridge, Mass.: De Capo Press, 2003.

Dann, John C., ed. *The Revolution Remembered: Eyewitness Accounts of the War for Independence.* Chicago: University of Chicago Press, 1983.

De Ridesel, Madame. *Von Riedesel, Friederike Charlotte Luise Freifrau. Letters and Journal Relating to the War of the American Revolution, and the Capture of the German Troops at Saratoga.* Translated by Jules Wallenstein. New York: G&C Carvill, 1827.

Ferling, John. *Independence: The Struggle to Set America Free.* New York: Bloomsbury Press, 2011.

Philbrick, Nathaniel. *Bunker Hill: A City, a Siege, a Revolution.* New York: Viking, 2013.

Raphael, Ray. *A People's History of the American Revolution: How Common People Shared the Fight for Independence.* New York: Perennial, 2002.

Savas, Theodore P. and J. David Dameron. *A Guide to the Battles of the American Revolution.* New York: Savas Beatie, 2006.

Stephenson, Michael. *Patriot Battles: How the War for Independence Was Fought.* New York: HarperCollins, 2007.

Volo, Dorothy and James M. *Daily Life During the American Revolution.* Westport, Conn.: Greenwood Press, 2003.

INDEX